Original title:
Through the Green Lens

Copyright © 2025 Creative Arts Management OÜ
All rights reserved.

Author: Simon Fairchild
ISBN HARDBACK: 978-1-80581-781-9
ISBN PAPERBACK: 978-1-80581-308-8
ISBN EBOOK: 978-1-80581-781-9

The Hush of Hidden Groves

In the shady woods, where squirrels chatter,
A rabbit hops by, and it's quite a clatter.
Trees wear their leaves like new summer hats,
While owls throw shade on the silly house cats.

Beneath the tall boughs, the mushrooms convene,
Throwing a party, it's quite the scene.
Frogs in tuxedos leap with such flair,
Dancing at dusk, without a care.

A chipmunk unveils his stand-up routine,
Cracking up turtles who nearly turn green.
With each little joke, they chuckle and snort,
As fireflies glow, they hold a court.

In this leafy kingdom, where whimsy won't end,
Nature's own jesters delight and pretend.
And when shadows grow long, all bid adieu,
Until next time, when the laughter rings true.

Canvas of Canopies and Skies

Up in the trees, the squirrels conspire,
To steal the birdseed, it's their great desire.
A party in the branches, a nutty ballet,
While birds tweet warnings, "Hey! Not today!"

The leaves have giggles, they dance in the breeze,
Tickling the branches, with such playful ease.
A canvas of green, splashed with sunlight bright,
Where nature paints laughter, from morning to night.

The Story of the Wild

Once a raccoon in a hat quite askew,
Attempted a heist for some leftover stew.
In a garden of veggies, he plotted and schemed,
But the carrots fought back, and the radishes screamed!

A tale of mischief, with a twist of delight,
Where the critters all giggle and frolic all night.
The tomatoes chuckled, they rolled on the ground,
As the raccoon retreated, a comical sound!

Whispers from the Orchard

In the orchard, the apples gossip and sway,
"Did you see the peacock? He strutted today!"
The pears share secrets, sweet as their flesh,
While bees buzz around, causing quite the mess.

Cherries chuckle, their laughter contagious,
While butterflies flutter, oh so outrageous.
A picnic of fruits, in laughter they bask,
Sharing tales of the sun, no need for a flask.

The Chorus of Climbing Vines

The vines twist and turn, in a line so absurd,
Singing their songs, though it's mostly unheard.
With tendrils of green, they reach for the sky,
Where the clouds roll their eyes and the birds pass by.

"Hey there, dear flowers, with your colors so bright,
Join in our rhythm, let's dance through the night!"
In this vine-covered world, all feelings align,
It's a rollicking romp, a botanical shrine!

Beneath the Boughs of Time

Beneath the branches, squirrels play,
Chasing their tails in a comical way.
The old tree chuckles, with arms spread wide,
Watching the antics of nature's pride.

Sunbeams dance like children at play,
Tickling the leaves that sway every day.
A grumpy crow gives a loud caw,
As a bee buzzes by, without a flaw.

Whispers linger in the breeze,
As gossiping leaves gossip with ease.
A chipmunk winks and buries a prize,
While daisies giggle under sunny skies.

Time ticks softly, with a greenish hue,
In this merry realm where laughter is due.
A picnic spread and laughter shared,
Beneath the boughs, few feel impaired.

Verdant Visions

In a patch of grass, a frog does croak,
Making funny faces, oh what a joke.
His friends just laugh and leap on by,
While the old willow waves a sigh.

Mossy patches hide secrets untold,
A snail wearing shades, feeling so bold.
But when the sun starts to break through,
He slips on a leaf, and oh, what a brew!

Caterpillars forming a quirky band,
Playing leaf drums, they take a stand.
Each note they hit makes the flowers sway,
Dancing along in their own silly way.

Through vivid shades of greens and gold,
Nature's humor slowly unfolds.
With every chuckle, the world feels bright,
In this whimsical realm, all is right.

The Leafy Labyrinth

In a maze of leaves, lost but found,
A band of ants marches, making a sound.
"Hey guys, left or right? We can't go wrong!"
Their tiny debate feels like a song.

A twist and a turn, they stumble awhile,
A bushy hedgehog starts to smile.
"Follow my lead, don't be such a mess,"
He rolls with laughter, no need to stress.

Overhead, a parrot shows off its flair,
Dropping nuts and giggles, without a care.
The lilting sounds of nature's jest,
Will have you chuckling, surely impressed.

Eventually, they find the exit above,
While the hedgehog offers a nod of love.
With friendships formed in the leafy round,
In this maze of laughter, joy is found.

Stories Woven in Ivy

Among the vines where shadows play,
A mouse tells tales of a daring day.
With every twist, a new plot unfolds,
In the book of life, excitement it holds.

A squirrel chimes in with a nutty quip,
Twirling around on a daring trip.
Oh, how the ivy listens with glee,
Hanging on tightly to each funny spree.

The tales bounce like bubbles in the air,
A butterfly pauses, stops to stare.
With giggles that flutter from bud to bud,
Nature's own comedy rises like flood.

As dusk approaches, the stories intertwine,
With laughter echoing like aged wine.
In this garden of whispers, secrets revive,
And ivy wraps warmly, where joy comes alive.

The Allure of Leafy Landscapes

In the woods I found my shoes,
Hoping they'd escape the snooze.
A squirrel chattered with delight,
Stealing snacks, what a funny sight!

The trees whispered all around,
Telling secrets without a sound.
A rabbit hopped with comic grace,
While I tripped over a hidden base!

Leaves danced in the bubbling breeze,
Chasing shadows, none would freeze.
A crow critiqued my fashion sense,
While I wondered if I made a fence!

Nature giggled, skies wore a grin,
As flowers bloomed, the bright folks win.
Amidst such fun, I rolled in grass,
Wondering how the bugs would pass!

Epiphanies in the Meadow

Among daisies, my thoughts took flight,
Where bees buzzed in a joyous plight.
I pondered life, with clover's aid,
But tripped over roots—how unafraid!

The butterflies danced without a care,
While I tried to take a proper stare.
Their colors flashing, bright and bold,
Made me feel a tad too old!

A sheep snickered, with a fluff so grand,
While I tried to draw, my pen in hand.
The grass tickled my nose, what a tease,
Made me laugh, saying 'Oh, please!'

An epiphany came adorned with fluff,
Life's too short; just have some fun stuff!
So I twirled amidst blossoms and cheer,
And waved to the ants sipping on beer!

The Swaying Symphony of Grass

In the field, the blades would sway,
As I tried to dance, fell on display.
A cricket chirped a funny tune,
While I swung my arms like a loon!

The sun peeked through a leafy arch,
Hosting a jazzy, grassy march.
With every step, my foot got stuck,
But the grass giggled, 'Hey, good luck!'

Rabbits hopped, doing their best show,
While I clumsily joined in, feeling low.
The melody of the wild was neat,
As I scrambled to keep my feet!

Rolling noodles on a grassy bed,
The world seemed silly, my worries fled.
It's a symphony of laughter and cheer,
In this field where I danced—oh dear!

A Lens of Nature's Serenity

The sun peeked in with a wink and grin,
As I wandered in calm, where chaos began.
Leaves wrapped around like a warm embrace,
While my thoughts raced, quickened the pace!

A frog croaked like a rockstar loud,
Drawn by his voice, I joined a crowd.
Nature's comedy show was on display,
With giggles at the antics, 'hip-hip-hooray!'

I found a snail moving so slow,
Said, 'Hurry up, we've places to go!'
While dancing daisies joined the scene,
Brought a breeze that felt rather keen!

Through this lens of serenity bright,
Every chuckle deepened the light.
So I laughed with the blooms and made a toast,
To the wild world and the creatures I love the most!

Fragments of Flora

In the garden, a gnome lays low,
His hat too big, he can't find his toe.
Plants giggle softly, in shades of green,
Whispering secrets, a leafy routine.

A daisy dances, twirling with flair,
While roses complain, 'This garden's unfair!'
Thorns give a poke, like a prickly joke,
Nature's ensemble, a laughter bespoke.

The Calm in Nature's Embrace

In the woods, where the sunlight breaks,
A squirrel sneezes, oh what a mistake!
Leaves shake with laughter, the branches sway,
As critters all giggle at the sneezing display.

A bunny hops by with a wiggle and bounce,
Chasing a butterfly, oh what a flounce!
Nature's own comedy, wild and absurd,
Each rustle and chirp, a whimsical word.

Vistas of Vivid Greenery

On the hillside, where the ferns are bright,
A lizard strikes a pose, thinking he's a knight.
He flexes his scales, all shiny and grand,
But trips on a pebble, oh what a stand!

The grasshoppers chuckle, in leap and in hop,
As the lizard regains his balance, a flop.
Nature's own theater, a vibrant display,
Where every mishap brings giggles our way.

Encounters with the Wild

Amidst the thickets, a bear tries to dance,
But stumbles right over a squirrel's last chance.
With a mighty 'thud', they collapse in a heap,
While birds above cackle, lost in their peep.

A deer roams nearby, contemplating its fate,
While trying to figure which way looks great.
With goofy confusion, it prances about,
In nature's own circus, laughter's a route.

The Verdure Within

In a patch of grass I lie,
A beetle walks and waves goodbye.
It seems so proud, a silly king,
Declaring this his favorite thing.

The daisies giggle, bend and sway,
While ants hold tiny parades today.
Each leaf whispers a juicy tale,
Of sneezes from a clumsy snail.

When sunshine flirts with vibrant greens,
Even weeds become ballet scenes.
A worm performs a wiggly jive,
In the soil where hopes arrive.

Oh, what a funny world we see,
In this garden, wild and free.
With laughter sprouting every hour,
Nature's jokes bloom like a flower.

A Walk Among the Ferns

I tiptoe through the leafy thrill,
Where ferns line up in perfect skill.
Each frond is like a waving hand,
Giggling softly as I stand.

A squirrel mocks with acorn flair,
While flowers toss their frilly hair.
The moss looks cozy, quiet, neat,
But underneath, a party's sweet!

What's that noise? A frog in tune!
Declaring, 'Hey! I own this room!'
With lily pads as splashing stages,
Their antics fill the book of pages.

So come and dance among the greens,
Where nature wears its playful jeans.
We'll laugh, we'll roll, we'll spin around,
In foliage, the joy is found.

The Color of Life's Essence

Chartreuse whispers, petals giggle,
While daisies play a little wiggle.
Orange leaves do a funky jump,
And crunchy twigs sing out a thump.

The violets wear tiny crowns,
With pins and needles for their gowns.
A bee buzzes, 'I run this scene!'
Pollen on his wings, how keen!

Every hue has a punchline bright,
In each shade, a thrill takes flight.
The sun picks out a color scheme,
Making sure it's quite the dream.

So join the vibrant riotous dance,
As flowers grin and grasses prance.
Together, in this vivid place,
We find pure joy in nature's grace.

In the Realm of Foliage

Welcome to this leafy show,
Where branches wave and petals glow.
The squirrels play the leading part,
While teasing trees with all their heart.

A berry bursts, then did you know?
It tickles when it starts to grow!
With laughter in each vine and sprout,
This realm of green's a joyous route.

Watch dandelions take a ride,
On breezes sweet, they glide and slide.
They scatter seeds like tiny stars,
Creating gardens near and far.

So wander in this wooded jest,
Where foliage comes to life, its best.
With smiles painted all around,
In nature's giggles, joy is found.

Glimmers Beneath the Mossy Veil

Beneath the moss, a creature peeks,
With tiny toes and playful cheeks.
It trips on roots, a dance of glee,
In leafy shade, where laughs run free.

A squirrel wears a dapper hat,
With acorns stored, he feels quite fat.
He slips and slides, a comic show,
And topples down with one loud whoa!

The ferns all giggle, swaying tall,
As raindrops tease, then start to fall.
They whisper jokes in breezy tones,
While critters giggle, all alone.

A turtle dons some shades of flair,
While frogs create a karaoke lair.
The mossy veil, a stage so grand,
Where nature sings a merry band.

Secrets in the Sunlight

Sunbeams peek through branches wide,
A ladybug takes a speedy ride.
She bumps a flower, it starts to sway,
And both of them giggle the day away.

A squirrel juggles acorns tight,
While bees buzz in with all their might.
"Hey, let's dance!" the blossoms shout,
And shake their petals all about.

The butterflies are having fun,
With colors bright, oh, what a run!
They flutter near, then zoom and dip,
A wild and whimsical friendship trip.

Secrets shared in golden rays,
While branches sway in sunny plays.
Nature's laughter fills the air,
With silly antics everywhere!

Portraits of the Overgrown

In corners lush where wild things sprout,
A gnome grins wide, without a doubt.
He poses proudly by the ferns,
While poky thorns attempt their turns.

A rabbit's ears stand tall in glee,
Wearing a crown made of fresh green brie.
He hops around, an artist's muse,
With weeds that wiggle in the hues.

The daisies freeze, they strike a pose,
While grasshoppers strike silly prose.
Each flower joins the fun parade,
In nature's gallery, they're unafraid.

The portrait speaks without a word,
Of wild adventures, often stirred.
With laughter painted on each leaf,
A world ablaze, beyond belief!

The Lush Veil of Memory

Memories rest in the thick green moss,
Where giggling shadows flit and toss.
Each tale untold beneath the trees,
Brings unexpected giggles on the breeze.

A chipmunk reminisces old games,
In fluffier cheeks, he stirs up names.
"Remember when we hid from rain?
Your acorn hat got stuck with grain?"

The river flows, with secrets past,
While frogs croak tunes that hold steadfast.
They leap and laugh through waters bright,
Creating echoes of pure delight.

The veil of green, a quilt of dreams,
With each stitch woven, as laughter beams.
Nature's stories, woven tight,
A tapestry of joy and light.

Traces of Life Beneath the Canopy

A squirrel stole my sandwich!
It climbed up the highest tree,
Chirping loud with glee, oh boy!
I guess lunch isn't meant for me.

The ants are throwing a feast,
They've invited all their friends,
Tiny tables made of leaves,
I hope my leg won't be the end!

A raccoon shows up in a mask,
Is he here for a costume party?
With a swagger, he digs through trash,
Looks like he thinks he's real hearty.

A snail just took forever, man,
I think he's lost or just too slow,
He shouts, "I'm just pacing myself!"
I laugh as he glides on his go.

The Breath of the Whispering Woods

The trees gossip like old friends,
As I trip over roots so sly,
Squirrels comment on my grace,
I swear I heard a little sigh.

A deer winks, I swear it's true,
I'm not sure if that's a good sign,
With a giggle, it bounds away,
And I'm left here sipping pine wine.

Mushrooms dance beneath my feet,
In a twirl, they start to sway,
"Join us!" they say, "Have some fun!"
I'd rather not, I'm on my way.

Birds are laughing at my hats,
They mimic each silly sound,
As I try to blend in here,
These woods are way too high-browed.

Essence of Emerald Journeys

In bushes thick with hidden jokes,
The frogs are croaking puns all day,
A fly, confused, looks for its path,
One leap, it's lunch—hip-hip-hooray!

The flowers wear their brightest hats,
While bees perform their tiny hum,
"Hey, what's buzzing?" one bee quips,
"Just work! But don't call us a bum!"

A toad struts by with great intent,
Claiming he's royalty, no doubt,
But tripping on his robe of moss,
Shows him what it's truly about.

Each root and leaf spins tales of fun,
Life below is full of cheer,
With nature's grin in goofy style,
I love it all—bring on the beer!

Discoveries in the Underbrush

What's that rustling in the grass?
Is it a monster? Or a cat?
Oh wait, it's just a hedgehog there,
Rolling like a little brat!

Old sticks are playing hide and seek,
They tell me secrets of the past,
But I just stepped on a twig,
Oops—my stealth skills are not so vast!

Lizards sunbathing on rocks,
Looking cool, they flick their tongues,
"Catch a fly! Or take a nap,"
I laugh at how nature has funs.

With mud splashes high on my shoes,
I wander in a wild parade,
Each squishy step a dance of joy,
In this green world, I'm unafraid.

The Forest's Quiet Gaze

Leaves whisper secrets, funny and bright,
Squirrels plot mischief, what a sight!
Trees wear their hats, all leafy and green,
Wondering what else could possibly be seen.

A raccoon in a cap, trying to blend,
Hiding from owls, his feathered friend.
The sun plays tag with shadows so wide,
In this nature circus, laughter can't hide.

Nature's Tapestry Unfolds

Butterflies flit, lost in a dance,
Chasing the bees, as if in a trance.
A frog croaks a tune, off-key but bold,
While ants carry crumbs, their story unfolds.

The flowers gossip, with colors so loud,
Wearing their blooms like a dazzling shroud.
In this colorful quilt, surprises do wait,
Nature's comedy show, truly first-rate!

Shades of Renewal

The clouds laugh softly, in shades of gray,
Dropping rain jewels in a playful way.
Puddles reflect, a carnival game,
In water mirrors, their joy is the same.

Sprouts poke their heads, with curious cheer,
Dressed in fresh coats, their debut is near.
Sunshine joins in, with a wink and a grin,
In this lively garden, it's hard not to grin!

Gazing at the Canopy's Secrets

Up above, the branches twist and twirl,
In the canopy's arms, the secrets unfurl.
A bird cracks a joke, with a chirp so keen,
While owls roll their eyes, they've heard it, I mean.

The rustle of leaves, a soft chuckle found,
Under this green roof, laughter abounds.
Nature's own theater, delightful and free,
With every glance up, more humor to see!

Fragrance of Fern and Blossom

In the garden, mushrooms dance,
Wearing hats, they take a chance.
Daisies giggle, watch them sway,
Holding hands, they like to play.

Bees in tuxedos buzz around,
Trying hard not to fall down.
While the tulips tell a joke,
Laughter rising like a smoke.

A snail slides in with a grand grin,
Says, "I'm here, let the fun begin!"
They cheer for ladybugs in flight,
As they twirl on, oh what a sight!

In this world of vibrant glee,
Nature's humor, wild and free.
For every bloom and tale well spun,
There's a laugh—come join the fun!

In the Heart of the Green

In the thicket, frisbees fly,
Squirrels chase, oh my, oh my!
A rabbit hops, with thrift store charm,
Wearing leaves as a little farm.

Amidst the shrubs, a band will play,
Frogs on drums have quite a sway.
Crickets sing with vibrant cheer,
Serenading all far and near.

A wise old owl runs the show,
Sipping nectar, acting slow.
Pulling jokes like seeds from dirt,
"In this green world, no one gets hurt!"

With every rustle, laughter grows,
Tickled by the breeze that blows.
For in this heart, wild jokes collide,
In the green, where glee won't hide!

The Warmth of Sunlit Leaves

Under sun, the branches sway,
Leaves lost in their merry play.
They whisper secrets with a twist,
Even thorns can't resist.

A woodpecker taps a beat,
With rhythm hard to skip or cheat.
While a lizard pretends to prance,
In its wild, eccentric dance.

Beneath a tree, a picnic waits,
Ants organize snacks on plates.
Giggles burst from all around,
As nature's humor does abound.

Sunlit laughter blooms like flowers,
Making memories for hours.
In this realm so bright and neat,
Funny moments can't be beat!

Echoes in the Thicket

In the woods, a bear tells tales,
With fishy swears and rainy gales.
He pulls a joke from his big hat,
While raccoons join in, just like that.

A deer pops up, a sidekick keen,
Says, "I'm here! You know what I mean?"
With every rustle, every caw,
The laughter echoes, fills with awe.

Underneath the tangled vines,
Critters gather, draw the lines.
Whippoorwill croons in laughter sweet,
Nature's chorus can't be beat!

As night descends, the fun stays bright,
With cozy home beneath the light.
In this thicket, laughter flows,
With every twist, a new joke grows!

Foliage in Focus

In the park, trees play peek-a-boo,
Their branches wave like they know you.
Squirrels dance, their tails in a swirl,
Nature's comedy with a leafy twirl.

A lizard laughs, sunbathing with glee,
While ants march on with their grand jubilee.
Even the flowers wear a silly hat,
Poppin' colors, just like a mat!

A Symphony of Leafy Hues

Leaves tap-dance in the autumn breeze,
Whispering secrets, much like teas.
A wind chime sings, as butterflies glide,
In this orchestra, there's no need to hide.

The branches twirl, in their leafy attire,
A comedy trio, like a quirky choir.
A beetle jesters, on a journey so grand,
Turning every pebble into a stage on land!

Reflections in the Meadow's Heart

Dandelions chuckle, looking quite fine,
As rabbits hop, in a comical line.
The daisies giggle, their petals so bright,
Bouncing around in the soft morning light.

A butterfly hiccups, in the warm sun's glow,
Landing on grass, for a quick little show.
Even the breeze joins in on the fun,
As nature winks, saying, 'We've just begun!'

The Spectrum of Nature's Eye

In this green world, mischief abounds,
Every branch hides giggles and sounds.
Leaves have debates on who's the most green,
While moss laughs along, playing unseen.

The flowers prance in their riot of hues,
Teasing each other with dazzling views.
A squirrel hosts a playful parade,
With acorns aplenty for all who invade!

Ferns and Wishes

Ferns in the forest dance so sly,
Wishing on leaves as breezes sigh.
A snail in a hurry, dreams of a sprint,
While grasshoppers laugh at his slow descent.

Whimsical whispers ride the air,
Frogs croak jokes without a care.
The trees are eavesdropping, just for fun,
As squirrels debate who could win a run.

Mossy pillows for sleepy heads,
In a game of tag, 'round a flowerbed.
Ladybugs giggle, plotting a scheme,
With their tiny crowns, they reign supreme.

In this jolly patch, all things twirl,
With butterflies gossiping in a swirl.
A dandelion puffs, "I wish for more!"
And sends its dreams wafting ashore.

Nature's Colorful Embrace

Painted petals pirouette in the glow,
Bees play hide and seek, a buzz in tow.
The tulips tell secrets to cheerful blooms,
While daisies create raucous little rooms.

Rabbits in bow ties dance on the grass,
Chasing each other for fun and sass.
A signpost reads, 'Chuckle Lane Ahead',
Where laughter sprouts from every thread.

In the pond, the fish wear little caps,
Playing chess on lily pads with maps.
A sunbeam slips on its golden shoes,
To join this party where nothing's on snooze.

Shade of the trees, a giggle fest,
Nature's embrace is surely the best.
With every color, there's joy to trace,
In this wonderland, we find our place.

Lurking in the Lush

In the thick of leaves, a shadow creeps,
A raccoon with schemes, as the laughter leaps.
He steals some berries, a gluttonous thief,
But chums with the owls, sharing light-hearted grief.

Frolicking fern fronds wave hello,
As butterflies waltz, putting on a show.
The woodpecker's drumming, a beat so bold,
With squirrels grooving, they can't be controlled.

Under the bushes, a hedgehog hides,
With tiny intrigue, where mischief abides.
Crickets recite, their poetry sly,
In this leafy kingdom, no need to be shy.

A parade of petals then takes the stage,
With the wind as their partner, they spin and engage.
Lurking in lushness, it's all quite grand,
Nature's clowns performing, hand in hand.

Sprouts of Spiral Dreams

Little sprouts spiral, reaching for light,
In their fanciful dances, a pure delight.
Worms tell tall tales to the roots below,
As they wiggle and giggle, putting on a show.

A sunflower grins, with a wink so wide,
"Join the dance," it calls, "let worries slide!"
While clouds play tag with the breezy air,
And frogs serenade with tunes, so rare.

Intertwined grasses weave a soft bed,
In dreams of the garden, all joy is fed.
With petals a-flutter, and laughter unfurled,
The sprouts of our dreams create a new world.

With each little sprout, we grow and play,
In this garden of giggles, let worries decay.
Nature's own dreamers, all sprouting bright,
In the spiral of laughter, take flight tonight.

The Palette of Perennial Life

In a garden where colors play,
The flowers argue night and day.
'I'm the brightest!' one claims bold,
While another just laughs, 'I'm gold!'

Bees buzz by with gossip grand,
'Have you heard? The roses are bland!'
Tulips tiptoe, prance, and sway,
As daisies giggle, 'Come what may!'

Grass blades tickle all the feet,
'Crabgrass, stop; that tickles, sweet!'
A little worm slips out to peek,
Cackling softly, 'Let's play hide-and-seek!'

What colors blend in nature's art,
Each hue with its own smart part.
A palette vast, of life and jest,
In laughter, blooms forever blessed.

Cradle of Flora's Heart

In the cradle where flowers dream,
Sunshine spills like honeyed cream.
Petals whisper a silly tune,
While butterflies dance, quite immune!

The daisies declare their beauty pageant,
But the thorns smirk, 'We're quite gallant!'
Every leaf plays peekaboo,
In this floral zoo, old yet new.

A bumblebee shows off his bling,
'Look, I found the latest spring!'
Sassy sprouts shimmy with glee,
Mimicking birds in a silly spree.

In laughter's embrace, they sway and twirl,
As pollen plays matchmaker, what a whirl!
In the cradle of nature's cheers,
Flora's heart beats loud, with no fears.

Notes from the Leafy Symphony

A leaf whispers, 'Listen here!
The frogs croak out, loud and clear.'
Crickets take their lead to sing,
While the toads hop, doing their thing.

'Faster, faster!' the mushrooms plea,
As squirrels dart up a tall tree.
Grasshoppers leap with mighty zest,
In this concert, they're the best!

The wind whistles a cheeky beat,
As daisies sway, tapping their feet.
'Let's dance!' declares a cheeky vine,
Stretching 'round, feeling just fine.

Nature's notes, a wild parade,
Each harmony a grand charade.
In this leafy realm so free,
Life's a giggle, come sing with me!

Nature's Secret Diary

In the pages of a soft green leaf,
Nature shares her comical grief.
'Oh dear sun, you're burning bright!
But I still can't get a tan just right!'

The squirrels write tales, bold and spry,
While butterflies flutter, oh so sly.
A sunflower snickers, 'I'm the best,
Have you seen my yellow chest?'

Thunderstorms spill their wildest plans,
'We'll wash away these stubborn tans!'
But then the rain slips in to play,
And puddles laugh at the dismay.

Leaves turn pages with a rustle,
In nature's world, there's always a hustle.
Writing laughs and giggles anew,
In nature's diary, forever true.

Gazing Beneath the Forest Veil

Beneath the trees, I spy a hare,
Dancing 'round roots without a care.
A raccoon in boots, oh what a sight,
Waving his paws, ready for a fight.

Squirrels are plotting, what can they find?
A stash of acorns, or perhaps my mind?
Whispers of leaves giggle with glee,
As I trip on branches, they laugh at me.

A fox with glasses reads a book,
About the best places for a cozy nook.
I join the fun, with a tree as my chair,
And share my snacks with those who dare.

So here I sit, with nature's jest,
In a world where critters are truly the best.
With a chuckle and cheer, I lose all strife,
In this green realm, filled with silly life.

A Tapestry of Herbaceous Hues

In gardens bright, where veggies play,
A carrot laughs, 'I'll win today!'
Tomatoes blush while onions cry,
The radishes wink, oh me, oh my!

The basil sings of pizza dreams,
As garlic dances, bursting at seams.
Peas in a pod tell corny jokes,
While broccoli dreams of grand folksy folks.

A sunflower strains to catch a peek,
Of bees in suits that go to sneak.
'Dinner's ready!' the kitchen calls,
While veggies chat behind the walls.

So let us roam this garden maze,
Where laughter grows in sunny rays.
Each herb and bloom, a tale that's spun,
In this vibrant world, we play and run.

Shades of Renewal

Spring's breath tickles the flowers bright,
They giggle and sway, oh what delight!
A daisy whispers secrets to the breeze,
While pollen dances with charming ease.

The tulips wear hats that twirl and spin,
Saying, 'Join us, come on in!'
A worm in sunglasses slides on by,
Claiming the sun, with a carefree sigh.

Caterpillars scheme their butterfly fate,
As ladybugs tell them to wait.
With shiny dots and colors galore,
They laugh at the bees who buzz and soar.

Nature's stage is a comical sight,
As critters frolic in morning light.
With blossoms that giggle and trees that grin,
In this playful realm, let the fun begin!

Secrets in the Thicket

In thickets thick, where shadows dwell,
A chubby raccoon rings the dinner bell.
He calls to friends in the moonlit glow,
'Let's feast on snacks that humans throw!'

A hedgehog rolling, stumbles with cheer,
'Catch me if you can!' he shouts with a sneer.
While fireflies twinkle, gossiping late,
In a world where partying won't wait.

The owls chuckle, wise and all,
Peeking from branches, heed their call.
'What's that ruckus, what's all the fun?'
With their sleepy blinks beneath the sun.

So join the frolic, oh come sustain,
In the secret thicket, there's no need to feign.
Where laughter echoes through the night,
In this leafy realm, we bask in delight.

A Whisper of Green in Every Step

With every footfall, grass does giggle,
A dance of leaves makes the branches wiggle.
The earth, it hums with a cheeky tone,
As ants parade like a marching bone.

The flowers wink in a colorful spree,
Drunk on sunlight, they giggle with glee.
A butterfly snickers as it takes a flight,
Dodging raindrops, oh, what a sight!

The mushrooms pop up to join the play,
Looking like umbrellas on a bright sunny day.
Nature's comedy unfolds with grace,
A laugh-out-loud show in this lush space.

So, take a step, join the mirthful run,
Life's antics unfold, let the laughter be fun!
In every nook, under each leafy crest,
A whisper of green holds nature's jest.

The Dance of Shadows and Light

The sun did peek through a leafy veil,
While shadows chuckled, a cheeky tale.
Bouncing sunlight and shadows quick,
A jokester game, nature's magic trick.

Squirrels skitter, all high and low,
Chasing giggles where the breezes blow.
The sun's bright laughter set the scene,
As shadows play hide and seek, so keen.

Leaves join the dance, in jittery sway,
Nature's party, come join the fray!
Footsteps echo, soft and spry,
As playful whispers drift on by.

The day whirls on, a merry spree,
With each silly sunbeam, feeling so free.
Come, share a chuckle, lighten your load,
In this light-filled kingdom, let fun explode!

Nature's Lush Embrace

In a velvet hug of emerald green,
Nature's laughter is sweet, yet unseen.
The daisies gossip, in a playful bunch,
While the bees buzz with a brunch-time crunch.

Leaves wave bye to clouds drifting past,
A ticklish breeze gives a squeal, so fast.
With each rustle and playful sigh,
Nature's embrace makes worries fly high.

Woodpeckers drum in a clumsy beat,
Playing in rhythm, oh, what a treat!
Frogs croak memes under moonlit spaces,
Making cheeky jokes with funny faces.

In this lush cradle, absurdity blooms,
Where laughter resounds in tree-filled rooms.
Join in the fun that wildness plots,
Embrace the green—give laughter a shot!

Balancing the Earth's Canvas

Nature's palette, so bright and zany,
With strokes of laughter—oh, isn't it crazy?
Tall trees wobble, layered in shades,
As mushrooms decide on fashionable braids.

Colors collide in a giggling spree,
Puppy-eyed flowers wave cheerfully.
Nature's quirkiness, let it unfurl,
As insects march on their own little whirl.

The sun throws paint with a jeering hand,
Making rainbows burst in this vibrant land.
The clouds play tag with the rooftops near,
Chasing the whispers, so silly and clear.

Nature's humor in a surreal dance,
Inviting all to join in the chance.
Balance is bliss in this colorful stance,
Where laughter blooms—it's a joyful romance!

Mornings in the Meadow

The grass is tickling my toes,
A squirrel's up to no good, I suppose.
Chasing shadows, hop and skip,
I'm a creature on a wild trip.

Dewdrops dance like tiny stars,
Butterflies hiding in marble jars.
Who knew the daisies could be so loud?
They giggle together, so very proud.

The sun spills forth a golden grin,
While ants march on like they're all kin.
"Just five more minutes!" I shout in glee,
But the cow gives me a stare, sarcastically.

Laughter echoes, a merry tune,
As I trip on a root like a cartoon.
Nature's comedy – oh what a show,
Rolling in laughter, I'll never outgrow.

Where Nature Paints the Sky

Look up! The trees wear their finest hats,
Branches swaying, chatting with the bats.
Clouds parade in a fluffy flock,
Dreamy shapes, like a friendly block.

Sunsets splash with colors so bold,
Orange and pink, stories untold.
Birds discuss their evening plans,
While crickets prepare their dance bands.

A cheeky squirrel throws down a nut,
"Catch this!" he shouts with a playful strut.
The wind whispers jokes in leafy tones,
As I sit back, laughing among the stones.

Stars start to peek, shy with delight,
Nature's jesters emerge for the night.
What a fine stage, the cosmos at play,
As the moon winks – "Isn't it a funny day?"

Sights from the Hidden Glen

In the glen where secrets roam free,
Lizards sunbathe, sipping on glee.
The brook chuckles as it flows,
Carrying whispers of long-lost woes.

I saw a frog with a top hat fair,
Claiming he's off to a fancy affair.
Dragonflies zoom like miniature kites,
Daring each other to fly to new heights.

The mushrooms conspire, a plan on display,
To turn the picnic into a play.
"Do this!" "Do that!" with a laugh they call,
As a mouse tiptoes, trying not to fall.

What a ruckus in the woodland space,
With nature's humor at a quick pace.
I scribble notes in mirth and zen,
Life's little wonders from the hidden glen.

Fluid Forms of the Flora

Wiggly stems in a dance so spry,
Petals whisper secrets, oh me, oh my!
Bumblebees buzz with annals of cheese,
While I wonder if flowers have knees.

Who knew daisies could do the cha-cha?
They twist and twirl like a fancy ballerina.
Sunflowers grin, standing tall with pride,
As violets blush at what's inside.

Buds poke fun at the roses' thorns,
"Are we really friends? Better not scorn!"
Laughter ripples through the leafy green,
Nature's comedy show, what a scene!

Flora's fluid forms, a sight so grand,
Polka-dots and stripes across the land.
In this wacky world, I smile and roam,
Among the blooms, I feel right at home.

Emerald Visions

In the park, a squirrel grins,
Wearing acorns like a crown.
He's planning a feast with his kin,
While I'm just looking down.

The grass tickles my lazy toes,
As daisies dance in the sun.
I swear I heard a flower propose,
To a bee, just for fun!

I saw a frog with funky shades,
Croaking tunes of sweet delight.
While ants march with parades,
Chanting "We rule the night!"

A breeze whispers silly tales,
Of trees competing for the best.
I chuckle at their leafy gales,
Nature's comedy fest!

Nature's Whispering Gaze

The wind tickles my ear,
As if sharing garden gossip.
A worm spins tales of the year,
On a lettuce leaf, it flips.

Bees buzzing secrets all around,
Roses blush as they retell.
The sun peeks through with sunlight sound,
And whispers, "All is well."

A hedgehog rolls, a barrel of fun,
Critters in a sporty relay.
Who knew nature could run?
I'm here just to watch them play!

A dandelion offers me tea,
"Careful, it's a bit wishy-washy."
I sip and feel so carefree,
With cheers from the mossy poshie!

The Verdant Perspective

The grass is greener, or so they say,
But it's just the same old turf.
A rabbit winks, doing ballet,
While I lose my picnic surf.

Butterflies sport their fancy attire,
Flirting with blooms in the light.
The bugs have plans to inspire,
With dances that dazzle the night.

A tree boasts its knots and its twists,
Claiming wisdom from ancient years.
But the crows caw, "Let's make lists!"
Of all the silly fears.

The clouds play peek-a-boo, oh so sly,
Painting shadows across the land.
While squirrels throw acorns up high,
Thinking they're just so grand!

Glimpses of a Leafy Realm

In the depths of a shady grove,
A snail tells tales of his races.
"Slow and steady!" he loves to grope,
While he moves at charming paces.

The trees gossip with each sway,
"Did you hear about the bloom?"
A flower blushes, has a say,
"I just made it through the gloom!"

The pond has a party with frogs,
Leaping high to a hidden beat.
With lily pads as the dance logs,
It's the hippest green retreat!

A curious raccoon peeks out,
Stealing snacks with a sly grin.
Nature's laugh, there's never a doubt,
There's fun where the wild things been!

Mosaics of Meadow and Stream

In a field where daisies dance,
The grasshoppers wear pants!
A butterfly on a quest,
Compares flowers to the best.

A frog sings in a silly croak,
Thinking he's a fancy bloke.
The river winks with a splash,
As it dreams of a future stash.

Squirrels gather acorn snacks,
While fitting into tiny slacks.
Each blade of grass, a tiny grin,
Echoes nature's playful spin.

Oh, what fun in this bright scene,
Where laughter is the routine.
A symphony of chirps and cheers,
Draws us close, erasing fears.

Green Serenity in a Shifting World

A leaf takes flight on a breeze,
Doing flips with utmost ease.
Painting portraits in the sky,
Where clouds morph into a pie.

The trees gossip in the sun,
About how the snails take fun.
While shadows stretch and tease the light,
Dancing shadows, quite a sight!

Bees wear hats, a funny sight,
Buzzing along with sheer delight.
Their tiny drones hum a song,
Join the party, it's not wrong!

In this charm of jumbled cheer,
Laughter grows from year to year.
As flowers bloom with goofy dreams,
All is bright, or so it seems.

The Language of Leaves

Leaves giggle in the sunlit glow,
Whisper secrets only they know.
With every rustle, a punchline formed,\nNature's laughter, a joy transformed.

Roots tell tales from deep below,
Of the world in a leafy flow.
While twigs compare their bristly styles,
And branches wave like happy miles.

Breezes carry the leaves' chatter,
"Did you hear?"—a joke, a splatter.
A chorus of rustles fills the air,
Nature's humour everywhere.

So we laugh at trees and blooms,
Life's antics fill all the rooms.
In green pastures, cheer is found,
With nature's smile—a silly sound.

Horizons of Overgrowth

In a jungle of mossy delight,
Tall tales twist in the morning light.
Where vines wrap up like a hug,
And caterpillars dance in a jug.

A lizard dons his tiny hat,
Claims he's a sleek and dapper cat.
The plants gossip like good friends,
Sharing secrets that never end.

Poke a stick at the roots so deep,
Watch them giggle, then creep and leap.
Shrubs wear glasses; they need to see,
Where the quickest path might be!

Each overgrown duty is a joke,
Nature's humor, it always pokes.
In horizons lush with green mistrust,
Laughter blooms, it's a must!

Shadows of Growth

In the garden where veggies dream,
Carrots dance in sunlight's beam.
Tomatoes gossip, green with glee,
While cucumbers plot, 'Won't you pick me?'

A leafy tree with a wooden grin,
Hides squirrels plotting mischief within.
They scurry and scamper, make quite a fuss,
Stealing snacks from our picnic bus.

The daisies chuckle, swaying light,
When bumblebees buzz, thinking they're bright.
"Oh dear," sighs one with a petal shake,
"Do they think we're flowers just for their sake?"

When rain drops fall, they twirl in delight,
Sharing puddles with frogs all night.
They sing and they play, not caring a bit,
For in nature's jest, they find their wit.

Vibrant Whispers of the Wild

The forest giggles under the sun,
Where every leaf shines just for fun.
A chipmunk shouts, "I'm fast as a flash!"
While clumsy raccoons tumble with a crash.

Flowers gossip in colors so bright,
"Who wore it best? Oh, what a sight!"
The daisies roll their eyes with flair,
As the poppies twirl without a care.

Butterflies flutter, playing tag in the breeze,
While ants march on like tiny soldiers with keys.
"Hey! Where's the party? We bring the snacks!"
"Follow the trail, just watch for the cracks!"

The brook babbles jokes, its ripples cheer,
"Why did the fish bring a suitcase here?"
For in nature's realm, hilarity reigns,
Where laughter is woven in sunlight's chains.

Nature's Living Palette

In the meadow where colors collide,
Bugs throw a party, what a wild ride!
A ladybug twirls, "Come join my spree!"
While a grasshopper croons, "Sing along with me!"

Sunflowers take selfies, striking a pose,
"Watch my best side, it's all that I chose!"
The bees roll their eyes, "Such vanity!"
"Just pollinate, friends! That's the plan, you see?"

The brook splashes cheerfully, "Let's splash and play!"
While fish flip and flop, bright as the day.
"Hey there, you splasher! That's way too cold!"
"I'm just trying to help!" says the fish being bold.

The trees whisper secrets, their leaves all a-flutter,
"Guess what, a squirrel just dropped my nutter!"
And with giggles and grins, nature holds its breath,
For in this wild canvas, joy knows no death.

Beneath the Green Canopy

Beneath the green where the shadows play,
The mushrooms giggle, they're here to stay.
"A game of hide and seek? Who's in?"
"Count to ten, and let the fun begin!"

The ferns whisper tales of days gone by,
"Remember the storm? We soared, we fly!"
While the spiders weave webs, intricate and bold,
"Look at my mansion! It's spun out of gold!"

A wise old owl hoots down with a grin,
"Why don't trees tell jokes? They'd crack the skin!"
While a bunny chimes in, "I just hop along,
To life's little melodies, that's where I belong!"

So the forest chuckles, a chaotic spree,
Where nature's jokes are wild and free.
In the embrace of the leaves, laughter ignites,
For every green moment, pure delight invites.

The Eye of the Leaf

A leaf on a branch, it can't really see,
But if it could talk, oh the gossip would be!
It'd share all the tales of squirrels up high,
And how birds get dressed in the silliest tie.

Whispers of wind tickle its veins,
Complaining of ants calling in their trains.
"Who needs a filter? I'm vibrant and free!"
A leaf with a laugh, so sprightly and spree.

Sunbeams come dancing, all golden and bright,
The leaf rolls its eyes: "More selfies, alright?"
With shade for a backdrop, it strikes a cool pose,
While others look on with some envy, I suppose.

Oh, to be green, in a forest so bold,
Where mossy adventures are waiting untold.
With every new drop of the dew on its side,
The leaf giggles softly, like nature's own guide.

Emerald Dreams in Twilight

At dusk when the forest turns soft and serene,
The moss starts to giggle, all fluffy and green.
"Why do we blossom, we're tripping on roots!"
Said a clump of bright ferns in long, leafy suits.

The fireflies flash with a twinkling delight,
"Turn on your glow, we're the stars tonight!"
But a twig remarks with a chuckle, so bright,
"I'd prefer a nap, then we'll laugh until light!"

When critters all gather for stories and tales,
Bouncing on mushrooms, like boats in the gales.
A rabbit, so witty, tells jokes about grass,
The laughter of nature, a joy none can surpass.

So here in the thicket where crazy things play,
Emerald dreams chase the worries away.
With rustling leaves as the giggly choir,
The forest is alive, and the jokes never tire.

Through Nature's Filter

A caterpillar dances, all limbs in a twirl,
"Plant parties are best; it's a leaf-laden whirl!"
The daisies all laugh, their heads bobbing low,
"Filter? We need none, we just steal the show!"

A frog croaks a tune with a silly old style,
While crickets join in, wearing wigs all the while.
"With every new sunset, we spark up our bling,
Nature's a feast, taste the joy that we bring!"

The flowers debate on who's the most bright,
While the daisies exclaim, "We're a pure delight!"
But twirling like petals upon the sweet breeze,
Is a wise old snail who's bringing the cheese.

So under the sky, with a sprinkle of stars,
Oh, nature's a party, no need for guitars!
All creatures unite, in this vibrant embrace,
And giggles erupt in this green, happy space.

Forest Reveries

In a nook of the woods where the wild throngs sway,
Stands a tree so wise, she's got something to say.
"I've seen all your antics, you mischief-makers,
What's next in your schemes, you leafy trouble-shakers?"

"A parade of the bugs, it'll happen at dawn!
With beetles in tuxes, and spiders in brawn!"
Said a bouncy old mushroom, brushing off dew,
"We'll cheer for the ants, in their tiny shoe crew!"

The wind starts to howl with a giggle and grin,
As the squirrels gather round for their nutty win.
They boast of their hobbies: acorn collecting!
While planning a jest that is sure to be wrecking.

When starlight joins in with a twinkly cheer,
The forest erupts; it's the laughter we hear.
With dreams made of green, in this whimsical space,
Where all of life's quirks find their true happy place.

The Verdant Path Untraveled

Upon the trail of thorns and leaves,
Frogs play chess under the trees.
Mice in hats sip herbal tea,
While rabbits giggle at the breeze.

A squirrel wears a tiny shoe,
Dancing wildly, catching dew.
With every step, a wild surprise,
Nature's jest is on the rise.

The path ahead is green and bright,
Yet still they wonder, what's in sight?
A picnic spread with ants and pie,
All join in a feast, oh my!

Laughter echoes, shadows blend,
In this wild world, there's no end.
So take a step, and don't delay,
Join the fun in Nature's play!

Glades and Gleams of Nature

In glades where sunlight flickers fast,
The mushrooms dance, a sight unsurpassed.
A raccoon spins in dazzling dress,
While crickets chirp, not one to mess.

Leaves rustle with a giggle sweet,
As chipmunks jive with nimble feet.
The flowers gossip, sharing dreams,
While ants debate their veggie schemes.

Beneath the boughs, the world is bright,
A carnival of charming light.
But heed the signs, do not dismay,
For daisies often steal the play!

With every turn, a zany sight,
Nature's wonders bring delight.
So skip along, with joy bequeath,
In these green glades, we laugh beneath!

Reflections of Tranquility

By the pond, the ducks all wear,
Fancy hats that dance in air.
While fish beneath in secret plot,
To steal the lure that someone's got.

The frogs recite their tales of woe,
What happened when they tried to croak.
Their stories turn from sad to bright,
As dragonflies take flight at night.

With laughter rippling, stillness breaks,
Nature knows how fun it makes.
Each leaf a page, each breeze a song,
A serenade where we belong.

Reflecting joys in every beam,
In tranquil waters, life's a dream.
So join the quack, the croak, the cheer,
And find your joy in the green sphere!

Illuminated by Nature's Brush

In fields where flowers paint the day,
An artist bee buzzes away.
With strokes of yellow, pink, and lace,
Creating smiles on nature's face.

A squirrel holding a tiny mug,
Sips acorn brew, snug as a bug.
While blossoms whisper secrets soft,
To cheeky winds that blow aloft.

The sun dips low, a golden grin,
As shadows shuffle, dance, and spin.
With every twirl, they make a mess,
Laughing loudly, what a jest!

So twirl and spin, let colors fly,
Join nature's whims, don't be shy!
For in this realm of vibrant rush,
Life's an art, a joyous hush!

www.ingramcontent.com/pod-product-compliance
Lightning Source LLC
Chambersburg PA
CBHW070327120526
44590CB00017B/2827

Beyond Glass and Gaze

A cat with big dreams sprawls on the floor,
Chasing shadows, his glory to score.
Curious ants form a parade so bold,
They stumble past tales of a great gold.

Clouds peek through and puff with delight,
"Is it almost dinner?" they muse in flight.
A rabbit in slippers hops with a grin,
Ears flopping proudly, just waiting to win.

The sun winks happily, a glowing friend,
Painting the world, what a colorful blend!
A squirrel, with a crown, declares it a feast,
As raindrops join in the fun, not the least.

"Hide and seek!" squeaks a mouse in a dash,
With a wave of tiny hands, he makes a splash.
In this lively scene, laughter takes flight,
Through the glass, we cherish the joyful sight.

Whispers of the Verdant View

A hedgehog spins tales of grass-court games,
While mushrooms gossip, comparing names.
Dewdrops giggle as they tickle leaves,
In this cozy corner where fun never eaves.

A dandelion puffs with a dramatic flair,
Revealing secrets, as they dance in the air.
Butterflies debating who can glide best,
In their neon robes, they flutter and jest.

The breeze brings news of a playful breeze,
Twirling around like it's teasing trees.
Jays cackle secrets like a cheeky crew,
Making time pass quickly in shades of blue.

As colors collide, a raucous show,
Each creature declares, "Let's steal the glow!"
In this verdant room of chuckles and cheer,
Nature's quirks make the funny things near.

Reflections on a Rain-Kissed Sill

Raindrops tap dance on the sill so bright,
As shadows of daisies twirl in delight.
The goldfish giggle, snug in their bowl,
Making waves at each droplet's roll.

A snail, with swagger, glides past the door,
Wearing a shell like a knight's heavy score.
Outside, the puddles are calling his name,
In a world where the laughter's a bubbling game.

The trees do the cha-cha in splishes and splats,
While worms humble-brag on their cozy mats.
Under the wetness, the sounds intertwine,
Creating a symphony, jovial and fine.

Behold the reflection where giggles collide,
Through laughter, the windows open wide.
In the rain's sweet embrace, we cast all our care,
As nature's own jester dances in air.

www.ingramcontent.com/pod-product-compliance
Lightning Source LLC
Chambersburg PA
CBHW070327120526
44590CB00017B/2826